REMARKABLE PEOPLE

Jonas Brothers

by Christine Webster

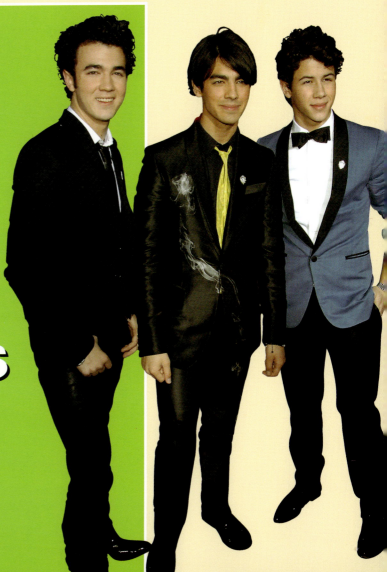

Published by Weigl Publishers Inc.
350 5th Avenue, Suite 3304, PMB 6G
New York, NY 10118-0069

Website: www.weigl.com
Copyright ©2010 WEIGL PUBLISHERS INC.
All rights reserved. No part of this publication may be reproduced, stored in a retrieval system, or transmitted in any form or by any means, electronic, mechanical, photocopying, recording, or otherwise, without the prior written permission of the publisher.

All of the Internet URLs given in the book were valid at the time of publication. However, due to the dynamic nature of the Internet, some addresses may have changed, or sites may have ceased to exist since publication. While the author and publisher regret any inconvenience this may cause readers, no responsibility for any such changes can be accepted by either the author or the publisher.

Library of Congress Cataloging-in-Publication Data

Webster, Christine.
 The Jonas Brothers / Christine Webster.
   p. cm. -- (Remarkable people)
Includes index.
 ISBN 978-1-60596-626-7 (hard cover : alk. paper) -- ISBN 978-1-60596-627-4 (soft cover : alk. paper)
1. Jonas Brothers (Musical group)--Juvenile literature. 2. Rock musicians--United States--Biography--Juvenile literature. I. Title.
ML3930.J62W43 2010
782.42164092'2--dc22
 [B]
                              2009005155

Printed in China
1 2 3 4 5 6 7 8 9 0   13 12 11 10 09

Editor: Nick Winnick
Design: Terry Paulhus

Photograph Credits
Weigl acknowledges Getty Images as the primary image supplier for this title. Unless otherwise noted, all images herein were obtained from Getty Images and its contributors.

Every reasonable effort has been made to trace ownership and to obtain permission to reprint copyright material. The publishers would be pleased to have any errors or omissions brought to their attention so that they may be corrected in subsequent printings.

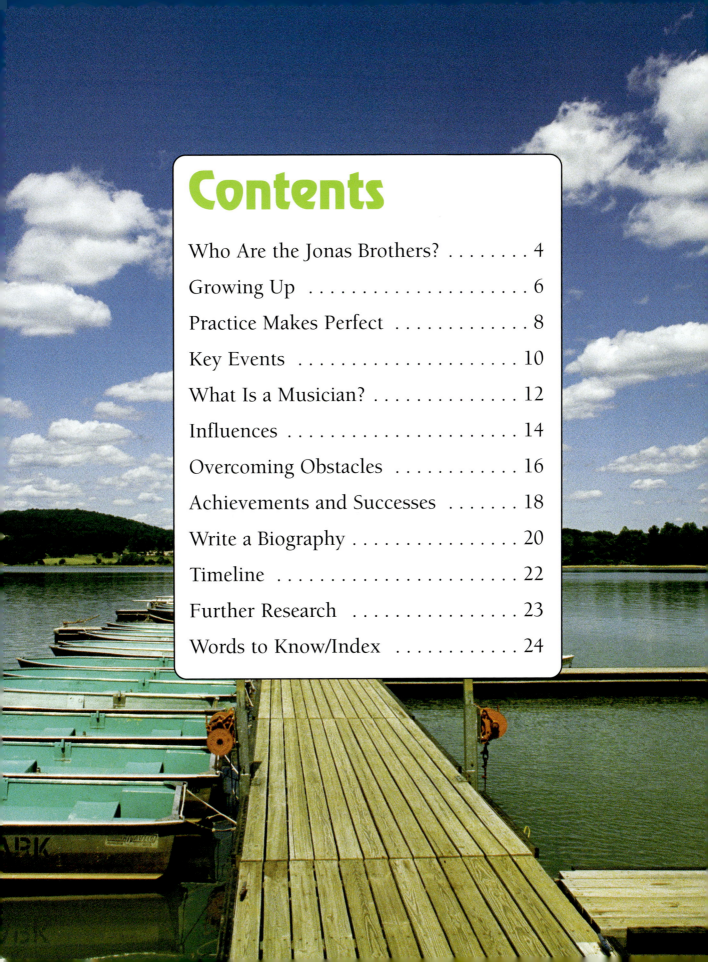

Contents

Who Are the Jonas Brothers? 4

Growing Up 6

Practice Makes Perfect 8

Key Events 10

What Is a Musician? 12

Influences 14

Overcoming Obstacles 16

Achievements and Successes 18

Write a Biography 20

Timeline 22

Further Research 23

Words to Know/Index 24

Who Are the Jonas Brothers?

With millions of fans, three successful albums, and a big-screen movie, the Jonas Brothers have earned a name as one of today's best-known musical groups. Kevin, Joe, and Nick Jonas began touring as a group in 2005, and since then, they have performed on stages around the world. In addition to playing music, the Jonas brothers have starred in TV shows and movies. Over the past few years, the brothers have achieved great success, and in 2009, they were **nominated** for one of the music industry's top honors, a **Grammy Award** for Best New Artist. With their friendly and outgoing image, the Jonas brothers have become popular with fans across the globe. To give back to their community, they use their fame to raise money and awareness of different **charities**.

> "For me, music is just life in general. When you walk outside, you start hearing beats wherever you go."
> -Kevin Jonas

> "There's always a way to find hope!"
> -Nick Jonas

> "[Singing] gets tiring, but...when you get back on that stage, it's worth every bit."
> -Joe Jonas

Remarkable People

Growing Up

Denise and Paul Jonas have four sons. Three of these boys, Joe, Nick, and Kevin, play in the musical group Jonas Brothers. Denise and Paul are musically talented and encouraged their sons to develop their own skills.

Paul Kevin Jonas II was born on November 5, 1987. He has the same first name as his father, but uses his middle name, Kevin.

Born on August 15, 1989, Joseph Adam Jonas thinks of himself as "the funny one." Joe loves to take pictures of his experiences touring the world with his brothers.

Though Nicholas Jerry Jonas is the youngest member of the band, he is thought of as its leader. Born on September 16, 1992, he is very serious and focused. The other Jonas boys have nicknamed him "The President."

■ Joe, Nick, and Kevin enjoy spending time with their younger brother, Frankie. Frankie is beginning his own musical career.

Get to Know New Jersey

FRUIT
Blueberry

FLAG

FLOWER
Common Violet

Thomas A. Edison invented the first light bulb in Menlo Park, New Jersey, in 1879.

The largest seaport in the United States is located in Elizabeth, New Jersey.

Les Paul of Mawah, New Jersey, invented the first **solid-body** electric guitar in 1940.

New Jersey is home to more horses per square mile than any other state.

The first organized baseball game was played in Hoboken, New Jersey, on June 19, 1846.

Think about it!

The Jonas brothers grew up around musicians and instruments. They learned how to play instruments very early in life. What special skills or hobbies are important in your family? Do your friends share any of these skills? In what ways can you put these skills to use?

Remarkable People

Practice Makes Perfect

Growing up, the Jonas brothers did not attend a regular school. Instead, their parents taught them their school subjects at home. The Jonas brothers also learned a great deal about music from their parents.

Though all three brothers were musicians, Nick was the first to work in the entertainment business. Nick's talent was discovered at the age of six, during a trip to a barbershop. He had been singing to himself while getting his hair cut. By seven, Nick began performing on **Broadway** in shows such as *A Christmas Carol*, *Les Miserables*, and *Beauty and the Beast*. He then began working on a solo album. By this time, Joe was performing on Broadway as well.

■ Paul Jonas, a former pastor, inspires strong values in Nick, Joe, Kevin, and Frankie.

One of Nick's songs was heard by staff at Columbia Records, and the company became interested in working with him. Nick released a few singles with Columbia, but they did not like his album. However, after hearing the three Jonas brothers sing together, Columbia decided to **sign** them as a group in 2005. The boys worked closely with Columbia producers on their album, and they soon began touring as a band. In the band, Joe and Kevin play guitar, Nick plays the keyboard, and all three brothers sing.

Being in the band takes a great deal of work. The Jonas brothers exercise to keep in shape. They practice their music often. Some days, they practice from when they wake up in the morning until they take the stage for a concert late that night.

QUICK FACTS

- Nick, Joe, and Kevin were inspired to write their song *Burning Up* after listening to the singer Prince.
- The Jonas brothers have named their tour bus "Bertha."
- When not playing real guitars, the boys enjoy playing the video game *Guitar Hero*.
- At first, the Jonas brothers thought about calling their band Sons of Jonas.

■ Before headlining their own shows, Jonas Brothers toured with other musicians, including Kelly Clarkson.

Remarkable People

Key Events

In August 2006, the Jonas Brothers' first album, *It's About Time*, was released. It did not sell very well, and Columbia Records ended their business deal. Hollywood Records produced the band's second album, and the song *S.O.S.* became the number-one selling track on iTunes. The success of the song tripled Jonas Brothers' album sales. By 2008, they were headlining a tour for their third album, *A Little Bit Longer*.

In 2007, Jonas Brothers had made the jump from music to television. They appeared on television shows, such as *Hannah Montana*, *Extreme Makeover: Home Edition*, and *Saturday Night Live*. Jonas Brothers also starred in a major television movie called *Camp Rock* in 2008. They have signed on to take part in another *Camp Rock* movie, along with their younger brother, Frankie. As well, a movie called *Jonas Brothers: The 3-D Concert Experience* was released in theaters in February 2009.

■ Jonas Brothers' first single, *Mandy*, was released in December 2005.

Thoughts from the Jonas Brothers

The Jonas brothers have outgoing personalities. They love to share their experiences with their fans.

Kevin talks about the difference between the brothers' first and second albums.

"The first one was us kind of coming into what the Jonas Brothers could be, whereas this one really shows off where we're at right now."

Nick's style is very important to him.

"A tie makes the outfit and shoes make the man."

Joe appreciates the culture of the different places he visits.

"My favorite thing about being on the road is the opportunity to travel and sightsee all over the world. I also really enjoy getting to meet our fans every place we go. It's fun to talk with people who speak all different languages."

Kevin enjoys spending time touring.

"The best part of being on the road for me is seeing the fans and brand-new places and faces every single day. On top of that, I get to do it while playing music. What could be better than that?"

Nick's older brothers looked after him when he was ill.

"On the way to the hospital, Kevin and Joe looked up diabetes online. They knew more about it than I did before I got there. They're there for me all the time."

Nick enjoys being on stage.

"The thing I like most about being on tour is being able to play a show every night. For me, that's one of the most amazing things in the world because I get to live my dream."

Remarkable People

What Is a Musician?

A musician is a person who can play an instrument, sing, or write music. Some musicians, such as the Jonas Brothers, have all three of these skills. Being a musician takes a great deal of work. Dedicated musicians spend many hours each day practicing their art.

Some musicians travel from place to place to perform. They try hard to write new songs that express their feelings and entertain their fans. When performing, musicians often develop a special style. This may mean dressing a certain way or producing a unique sound.

■ Some musicians, such as the Jonas Brothers, are paid for their skill. Others sing, perform, or write music for fun.

Musicians 101

Miley Cyrus (1992–)

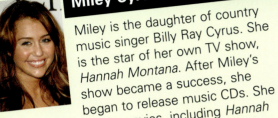

Miley is the daughter of country music singer Billy Ray Cyrus. She is the star of her own TV show, *Hannah Montana*. After Miley's show became a success, she began to release music CDs. She has also starred in movies, including *Hannah Montana*. Miley was nominated for a Golden Globe and Critic's Choice Award for her song *I Thought I Lost You*. She was named one of *Time Magazine*'s 100 Most Influential People in the World in 2008.

Jesse McCartney (1987–)

Jesse is a singer, songwriter, and actor. He began singing and acting when he was seven years old, and was known across the United States by the time he was 10. Jesse sang in the group Dream Street before releasing albums of his own. He has acted and done **voice-overs** in several Disney films. Jesse plays for his fans at shows across the country.

Justin Timberlake (1981–)

Justin began his career with the group 'N Sync. After singing with that group for seven years, Justin released his first solo album. To date, *Justified* has sold more than seven million copies around the world. Since then, he has released another album and worked with other artists on group projects. Justin has performed and recorded with artists such as Janet Jackson, Madonna, Timbaland, The Neptunes, and 50 Cent. He is part-owner of two New York restaurants, produces a clothing line, and has had roles in movies.

Taylor Swift (1989–)

Taylor is a country singer with a pop sound. Her first single, called *Tim McGraw* for the country singer of the same name, went to number six on the music charts soon after it was released. She released her first album in 2006 and another in 2008. In 2008, Taylor was the top-selling country artist in the United States. Her two albums sold more than four million copies. Taylor's second album stayed at the top of the charts longer than any other female country artist's album.

Musical Instruments

All musicians are skilled at playing some sort of instrument. Instruments are devices that produce musical notes when played by people. They can be as simple as a recorder or as complex as a grand piano. Many popular bands use guitars. These six-stringed instruments can be strummed or plucked to make notes. When more than one note is played at a time, this is called a chord. Notes and chords from different instruments are combined to make a song.

Remarkable People

Influences

One of the main influences for all three Jonas brothers is their family. The Jonas family keeps the boys grounded. They help the boys to stay focused on their music and their long-term goals. The brothers have especially strong ties to their father.

All three Jonas brothers are influenced by the music of Elvis Costello and Johnny Cash. However, each brother has his own musical influences. Kevin is inspired by country music. He loves how country songs often tell stories and wants his music to do the same. Kevin's favorite country singers are Keith Urban and Garth Brooks. He also enjoys the music of Stevie Wonder and John Mayer. Seeing and hearing John play is one of the reasons Kevin began playing the guitar.

Joe's influences include The Strokes and the Rolling Stones. He has said that Mick Jagger of the Rolling Stones is one of his heroes. Joe tries to bring some of Mick's style to his own performances.

■ Listening to the band Oasis gave Joe the idea to use a tambourine in some of the band's songs.

Nick has said that the one rock musician he would most like to talk with over dinner is Paul McCartney. Paul was a member of The Beatles, one of the most successful bands of all time. Paul also led the band Wings and has had a long and successful solo career. Nick would like to hear Paul tell stories about his music and performances. Nick also is influenced by the artist Prince.

THE BONUS JONAS

Frankie Jonas was born on September 28, 2000. His older brothers call him the "Bonus Jonas." Frankie is a musician as well, and plays the drums. He has his own band called Hollywood Shake-Up. One day, he says, Joe, Kevin, and Nick will play as an opening act for his band. Frankie is becoming more involved with Jonas Brothers as time goes on. He has been on screen in the Jonas Brothers' TV show, as well as their 3-D concert movie. Frankie has also joined the cast of the second *Camp Rock* movie. The animated film, *Ponyo on the Cliff by the Sea* features Frankie as the voice of one of the characters.

■ Frankie often attends events with his three older brothers.

Remarkable People

Overcoming Obstacles

Along with their success, the Jonas brothers have had to overcome many obstacles. In November 2005, Nick began to lose a great deal of weight. The band had been touring, and his mother thought Nick had been working too hard. The brothers decided to take a break. Nick went to a doctor and learned he had Type 1 diabetes.

Diabetes is a disease that keeps people from digesting food properly. People with diabetes have trouble moving sugar to where it is needed in the body. The body breaks down food into sugar for energy. This sugar enters the blood and is pumped to where the body needs energy.

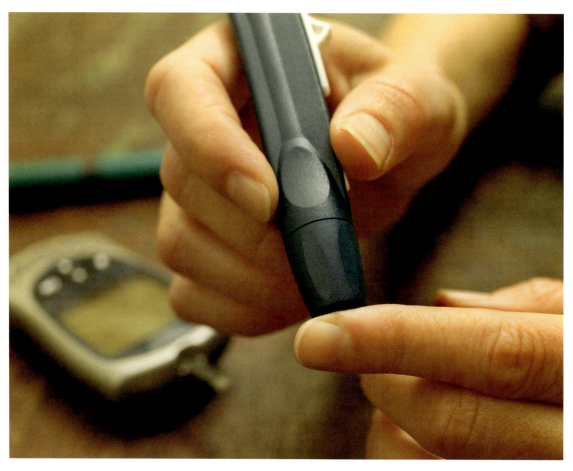

People who have diabetes use a special meter to check their blood sugar level.

When a person has diabetes, sugar builds up in the blood. Too much sugar in the blood can cause serious illness. Diabetes is controlled by injecting **insulin**. This is the chemical the body needs to help it move sugar properly. Insulin injections allow people with diabetes to live active lives.

Hearing the news of Nick's illness was a shock to the family. Nick spent a few days in the hospital. He learned to monitor his blood sugar levels and the foods he ate.

■ Each of the brothers wears a purity ring as a symbol of their promise to behave as role models.

Remarkable People 17

Achievements and Successes

Since Jonas Brothers first released *It's About Time*, the band has received many awards and nominations. In 2008, their popularity helped them sweep the Teen Choice Awards. Jonas Brothers won for Choice Breakout Group, Choice Male Red Carpet Icons, Choice Hotties, Choice Music Single, Choice Love Song, and Choice Summer Song. They were also nominated for having the Most Frantic Fans.

In 2008, MTV recognized Jonas Brothers for their most popular song from *A Little Bit Longer*, *Burning Up*. The video for this song was nominated for Best Video of the Year and Best Pop Video.

■ At the 2009 Grammy Awards, Jonas Brothers performed with Stevie Wonder.

Other countries have started to take notice of the Jonas Brothers as well. MTV Latin America chose the Jonas Brothers as Best International Pop Artists. The French radio group NRJ chose Jonas Brothers as the Best International New Artist.

In addition to their music, the Jonas brothers have also released several successful DVDs of their concerts. They also have a book called *Burning Up: On Tour with the Jonas Brothers*. It shows what goes on behind the scenes of a Jonas Brothers tour.

One of the Jonas Brothers' career highlights was performing at the Kids **Inaugural** Concert to celebrate Barack Obama's swearing in as president. A few days later, the brothers surprised the president's daughters, Malia and Sasha, by playing at a party at the White House.

CHANGE FOR THE CHILDREN FOUNDATION

Inspired by Nick's struggle with diabetes, the Jonas brothers began the Change for the Children Foundation. They created this charity to give their young fans the chance to help other kids their age who are in need of medical care. The money collected by Change for the Children goes to charities such as the American Diabetes Association and the St. Jude Children's Research Hospital. In addition to the money collected by the foundation, the Jonas brothers also give 10 percent of everything they earn to churches and charities.
www.changeforthechildren.org

Remarkable People

Write a Biography

A person's life story can be the subject of a book. This kind of book is called a biography. Biographies describe the lives of remarkable people, such as those who have achieved great success or have done important things to help others. These people may be alive today, or they may have lived many years ago. Reading a biography can help you learn more about a remarkable person.

At school, you might be asked to write a biography. First, decide who you want to write about. You can choose musicians, such as the Jonas brothers, or any other person you find interesting. Then, find out if your library has any books about this person. Learn as much as you can about him or her. Write down the key events in this person's life. What was this person's childhood like? What has he or she accomplished? What are his or her goals? What makes this person special or unusual?

Jonas Brothers

A concept web is a useful research tool. Read the questions in the following concept web. Answer the questions in your notebook. Your answers will help you write your biography review.

Timeline

YEAR	JONAS BROTHERS	WORLD EVENTS
1987	Kevin Jonas is born.	Aretha Franklin is inducted into the Rock and Roll Hall of Fame. She is the first woman to receive this honor.
1989	Joe Jonas is born.	Paul McCartney releases an album only in the USSR. Unofficial copies sell for $1000 in other parts of the world.
1992	Nick Jonas is born.	Nirvana's *Nevermind* album reaches number one on the *Billboard* charts.
2005	Nick is diagnosed with Type I Diabetes.	Mariah Carey's album, *The Emancipation of Mimi*, reaches number one on the charts immediately after its release.
2006	Jonas Brothers release their first album.	Tickets go on sale for Madonna's *Confessions* tour and sell out within hours.
2007	Jonas Brothers perform at the American Music Awards.	Radiohead releases their *In Rainbows* album online. Fans pay what they want to download the music.
2008	The movie *Camp Rock* is released.	The New Kids on the Block release their first album in 15 years.
2009	Jonas Brothers are nominated for a Grammy Award for Best New Artist.	Katy Perry wins the BRIT Award for International Female Solo Artist.

Further Research

How can I find out more about the Jonas brothers?

Most libraries have computers that connect to a database that contains information on books and articles about different subjects. You can input a key word and find material on the person, place, or thing you want to learn more about. The computer will provide you with a list of books in the library that contain information on the subject you searched for. Non-fiction books are arranged numerically, using their call number. Fiction books are organized alphabetically by the author's last name.

Websites

For news and information about Jonas Brothers, visit
http://www.jonasbrothers.com/

To learn about the *Camp Rock* movie, visit
http://tv.disney.go.com/disneychannel/originalmovies/camprock

Remarkable People

Words to Know

Broadway: musical theater that runs in New York City

charities: groups that collect money to help people in need

Grammy Award: the United States' top award for popular music

inaugural: marking the begining of an activity

insulin: a chemical that keeps the amount of sugar in the blood steady

nominated: added to a small list of people who will be considered for awards

sign: to agree to work with a music company for a set period of time or number of albums

solid-body: an electric guitar without a hollow body

voice-overs: provides the voice of a character in an animated movie or video game

Index

A Little Bit Longer 10, 18
Burning Up 9, 18, 19
Camp Rock 10, 15, 22, 23
Columbia Records 9, 10
Cyrus, Miley 13
diabetes 11, 16, 17, 19, 22
Grammy Award 4, 18, 19
instrument 7, 12, 13
Jonas, Denise 6
Jonas, Frankie 6, 8, 10, 15
Jonas, Paul 6, 8
McCartney, Jesse 13
Swift, Taylor 13
Timberlake, Justin 13
Wonder, Stevie 14, 18